Sports Illustrated KIDS

Prime Time Plays

HOCKEY'S WICKEDEST GOALS!

by Matt Doeden

CAPSTONE PRESS
a capstone imprint

Capstone Captivate is published by Capstone Press, an imprint of Capstone.
1710 Roe Crest Drive, North Mankato, Minnesota 56003
www.capstonepub.com

SPORTS ILLUSTRATED KIDS is a trademark of ABG-SI LLC. Used with
permission.

Library of Congress Cataloging-in-Publication Data
Names: Doeden, Matt, author.
Title: Hockey's wickedest goals! / by Matt Doeden.
Description: North Mankato, Minnesota : Capstone Press, 2021. | Series: Sports
    illustrated kids prime time plays | Includes bibliographical references and index. |
    Audience: Ages 8-11 | Audience: Grades 4-6 | Summary: "Whack! When the blade
    strikes the puck, it's prime time on the ice. From sizzling slap shots to brilliant
    backhands, experience the wickedest goals from hockey's biggest superstars. These
    sensational shots were so hot, they practically set the ice on fire!"—Provided by
    publisher.
Identifiers: LCCN 2020025090 (print) | LCCN 2020025091 (ebook) | ISBN
    9781496695345 (library binding) | ISBN 9781496696908 (paperback) | ISBN
    9781977154330 (pdf)
Subjects: LCSH: Hockey—History—Juvenile literatue.
Classification: LCC GV847.25 .D646 2021 (print) | LCC GV847.25 (ebook) | DDC
    796.356—dc23
LC record available at https://lccn.loc.gov/2020025090
LC ebook record available at https://lccn.loc.gov/2020025091

Image Credits
Alamy: Tribune Content Agency LLC, 15; AP Images: Eric Draper, bottom 25, Paul
Connors, 29; Getty Images: Al Bello, 23, B Bennett, 7, 20, 28, Bruce Bennett, 18, Graig
Abel, 21, Gregg Forwerck, bottom 17, Icon Sportswire, top 17, 19, Len Redkoles, 26,
Robert Beck, top 25; Newscom: Gary Hershorn, 10; Shutterstock: BK_graphic, design
element, Eugene Onischenko, Cover; Sports Illustrated: David E. Klutho, 5, top 13,
Heinz Kluetmeier, 9, Neil Leifer, 8, Robert Beck, bottom 13

Editorial Credits
Editor: Christopher Harbo; Designer: Sarah Bennett; Media Researcher: Eric Gohl;
Production Specialist: Katy LaVigne

All internet sites appearing in back matter were available and accurate when this
book was sent to press.

Printed and bound in the USA.   PO 3837

TABLE OF CONTENTS

INTRODUCTION
GOAL! 4

CHAPTER 1
GAME CHANGERS 6

CHAPTER 2
JAW-DROPPERS 14

CHAPTER 3
UNFORGETTABLE GOALS 20

GLOSSARY 30
READ MORE 31
INTERNET SITES 31
INDEX 32

Words in **bold** are in the glossary.

GOAL!

The crowd roars as the clock ticks down. A skater takes control of the puck at center ice. He charges across the **blue line** and weaves through defenders. He draws his stick back and fires a lightning-fast shot.

The goalie tries to react. But it's too late. The puck zips past his glove and into the corner of the net. Goal!

Michal Handzuš flicks the puck over the outstretched arm of Boston Bruins goalie Tuukka Rask to score a goal for the Chicago Blackhawks in the 2013 Stanley Cup Finals.

No sport can match that fast-paced action of hockey. Fans love cheering on great saves, bone-rattling **checks**, and pinpoint passes. But nothing gets them more excited than a big goal. What makes a goal great? Sometimes it's the situation. An **overtime** winner or a playoff clincher is hard to forget. Sometimes it's the difficulty. Flying, spinning, backhanded shots thrill fans and players alike. Read on to learn more about some of the wickedest goals in the history of the sport.

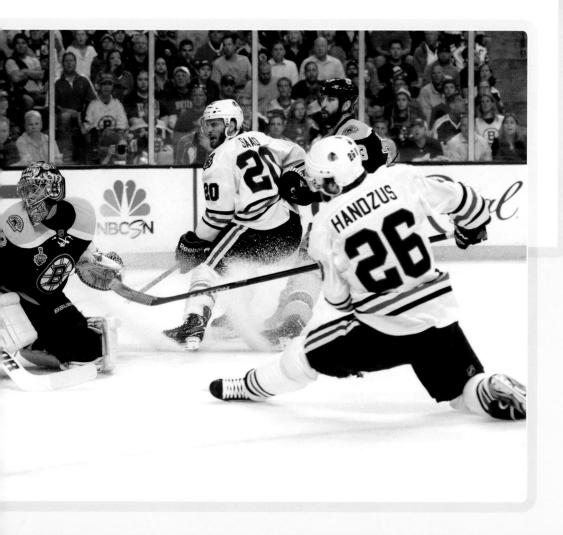

CHAPTER 1

GAME CHANGERS

Some of the biggest shots come when the game is on the line. Check out some of the most remarkable game-changing shots in hockey history.

Orr's Flying Goal

The Boston Bruins needed just one more victory. It was Game 4 of the 1970 Stanley Cup Finals. Boston fans were hungry for a championship. The team hadn't won one in 29 years.

Boston trailed St. Louis in the third period. But they charged back to tie the game at 3–3 and force overtime. Just 40 seconds into the overtime period, Bruins **defenseman** Bobby Orr got control of the puck. He passed it to teammate Derek Sanderson. Orr never stopped moving. He charged toward the net.

Sanderson quickly slid the puck back to Orr. A St. Louis defender tripped Orr as he streaked in front of the goal. Orr flew through the air as he got off the shot. The puck sailed into the net. The thrilling goal clinched the series for Boston. The long wait was over, thanks to one of the most amazing goals in National Hockey League (NHL) history.

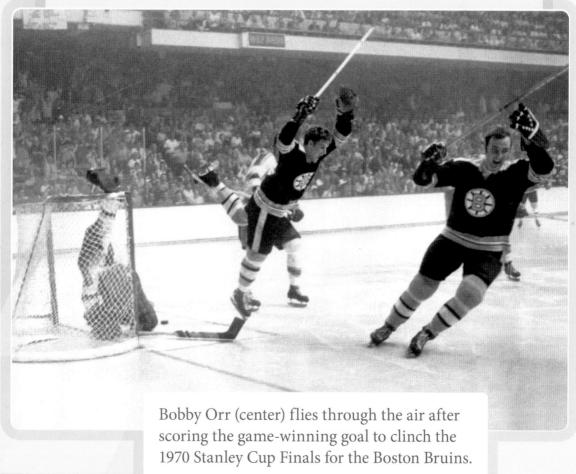

Bobby Orr (center) flies through the air after scoring the game-winning goal to clinch the 1970 Stanley Cup Finals for the Boston Bruins.

Miracle

Team USA was not supposed to win gold at the 1980 Winter Olympics. That's because the Soviet Union's team was bigger, faster, and more experienced. The Soviets had not lost an Olympic hockey game since 1968. They had crushed every team they had faced. Most experts expected them to crush the young Americans in the semifinal round too.

But Team USA surprised everyone. They trailed by just one goal in the third period. Mark Johnson tied it with about 12 minutes left to play. Less than two minutes later, the puck came loose in the Soviet zone. Mike Eruzione collected it and rifled a long shot. The puck buzzed just inside the pipe. Goal!

Mike Eruzione's shot slides into the net to give Team USA a 4-3 lead against the heavily favored Soviet Union team in the semifinal round of the 1980 Winter Olympics.

Team USA held on to win the game. They went on to beat Finland for the gold medal. The Miracle on Ice remains one of the biggest moments in Winter Olympic history.

Team USA celebrates their miraculous win over the Soviet Union to move on to the gold medal round against Finland.

Mike Eruzione became a hockey legend with his goal. But he did not go on to play in the NHL. His Olympic gold medal marked the end of his hockey career.

Walkoff Winner

The 2000 Stanley Cup Finals was a series of long battles. The Dallas Stars won Game 5 in triple overtime. Then Game 6 went to double overtime. The New Jersey Devils needed a goal to finish out the series.

About eight minutes into the second overtime, the Devils were on the attack. A loose puck slid into the corner of the Dallas zone. Winger Patrik Eliáš hurried to retrieve it. As he did, center Jason Arnott skated out in front of the goal.

Dallas Stars goalie Ed Belfour can't stop Jason Arnott's blazing shot to win the 2000 Stanley Cup for the New Jersey Devils.

Without turning around, Eliáš slid a backward pass in front of the net. Arnott lined up and fired a hard **one-timer**. Goaltender Ed Belfour couldn't get there in time to stop it. The Devils stormed the ice to celebrate their championship. It was one of the greatest goals—and passes—in Stanley Cup history.

Oh Canada!

The gold medal at the 2010 Winter Olympics came down to a battle between two powerhouses. The United States and Canada put on one of the greatest shows in Olympic hockey history. Regulation ended in a 2–2 tie. It was **sudden death** to crown the champion.

Seven minutes into the overtime, Canada took control of the puck. Sidney Crosby weaved his way into the Team USA zone. Crosby fired a quick shot. Goaltender Ryan Miller deflected it.

Crosby tracked down the puck in the corner. He passed it to Jarome Iginla. Then he skated toward the net. The defense collapsed on Iginla. As he fell to the ice, he punched the puck back to Crosby. Crosby fired. This time, Miller couldn't stop it. Canada celebrated its gold medal, and Crosby became an Olympic legend.

FACT

Canada has won nine gold medals in men's ice hockey. That's the most in Olympic history. Canada's women also lead the way with four Olympic gold medals.

Team Canada celebrates Sidney Crosby's game-winning overtime goal (top) before gathering for a photo with their 2010 Olympic gold medals (bottom).

CHAPTER 2

JAW-DROPPERS

The world's best players can do amazing things with the puck. Read on to learn more about some of the most amazing and **acrobatic** shots in hockey history.

Between the Legs

Some goals are all power. Some come from great teamwork. Others are just luck. On October 16, 2019, Columbus Blue Jackets forward Sonny Milano scored a goal that was pure style.

Milano got the puck on a **breakaway** in the third period. Two Dallas Stars defenders tried to slap the puck away as Milano skated toward the goal. Milano calmly tapped the puck back between his legs. He turned his body. With his stick between his legs, he flipped an amazing backhand right into the net. It was a thing of beauty, and it helped the Blue Jackets to a 3–2 victory.

Sonny Milano shows off his stick skills with a backhand shot from between his legs to score a goal against the Dallas Stars.

Lacrosse Style

The NHL has been around for more than a century. So it's hard to do something new. But that's what Carolina Hurricanes winger Andrei Svechnikov did on October 29, 2019.

Carolina trailed the Calgary Flames 1–0 in the third period. Svechnikov skated with the puck behind the Carolina net. Svechnikov stopped and turned his body. He scooped up the puck onto the blade of his stick. Then he wrapped it around and stuffed it into the top corner of the goal. His "lacrosse-style" goal was the first in the history of the NHL. Svechnikov went on to score the game-winning goal three minutes later. What a night!

FACT

One lacrosse-style goal wasn't enough for Svechnikov. He scored a second one the same way against the Winnipeg Jets on December 17, 2019.

Andrei Svechnikov lifts the puck with the blade of his stick to flip it past the goalie (top) and then celebrates his lacrosse-style goal. (right).

Crosby up to Bat

Sidney Crosby looked like a baseball player for a moment during the 2018 playoffs. Crosby and the Pittsburgh Penguins led the Philadelphia Flyers 4–0 in their first playoff game. The Penguins were on a rush in the second period, looking to add to their commanding lead.

The National Women's Hockey League

The National Women's Hockey League (NWHL) is a women's pro hockey league. It started play in 2015. Each year, teams compete for the Isobel Cup. Through 2020, Jillian Dempsey is the league's all-time goal-scoring leader. She has scored 46 goals in NWHL play.

Kelli Stack (61) of the Connecticut Whale and Brooke Ammerman (20) of the New York Riveters battle as they race across the ice.

Brian Dumoulin blasted a slap shot toward the goal. But a defender deflected it. The puck fluttered and spun through the air. It went toward Crosby, near the post. Crosby did the only thing he could. He lifted his stick and took a baseball-style swing at it. And it worked! Crosby whacked it past goalie Brian Elliott for one of the most jaw-dropping goals fans had ever seen.

Sidney Crosby (87) takes a swing at the puck to bat it past the goalie and into the net for a one-of-a-kind goal.

UNFORGETTABLE GOALS

Some goals just stand out. They're the unusual, the record-breaking, and the **milestone** markers. Check out these unforgettable goals.

Goalie Goal

Goalies aren't supposed to score goals in the NHL. But on December 9, 1987, that's what Ron Hextall of the Philadelphia Flyers did.

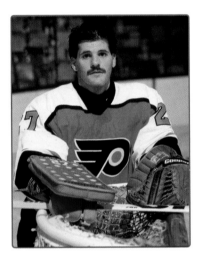

Ron Hextall

The goal came in the final moments of a game against the Boston Bruins. Philly led 4–2. Boston pulled its goaltender for an extra skater. The puck came deep into the Philly zone. Hextall tracked it down. He fired it the length of the ice toward the empty net. Somehow, the puck got through all six Boston skaters and slid into the empty net. It was the first time an NHL goalie had ever shot the puck directly into the opposing net. The next season, he did it again in a playoff game!

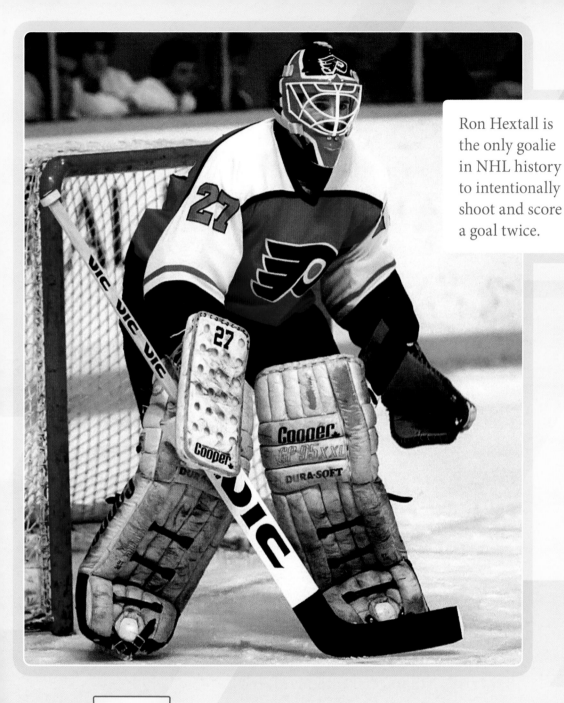

Ron Hextall is the only goalie in NHL history to intentionally shoot and score a goal twice.

FACT

The Montreal Canadiens have won the Stanley Cup 24 times. That's the most in NHL history. The Toronto Maple Leafs are second with 13 titles.

Nolan Calls His Shot

NHL All-Star games feature the best talent in the world. So it's no surprise that one of the most memorable goals in history came during the 1997 All-Star Game.

Owen Nolan was the star of the game. In the second period he scored two goals just eight seconds apart! But somehow, he topped that in the third period. Nolan controlled the puck on a breakaway. As he sped toward goalie Dominik Hašek, Nolan pointed at the top-right corner of the goal. Then he drew back his stick and fired a shot, exactly where he'd pointed. Nolan called his shot, then he delivered. It was an unforgettable way to complete the **hat trick**. Nolan celebrated with his teammates as fans threw hats onto the ice.

Owen Nolan raises his arms in celebration after calling and then making the shot that completed his hat trick in the 1997 All-Star Game.

Gretzky Scores #802

No player has scored more NHL goals than Wayne Gretzky. "The Great One" broke Gordie Howe's record of 801 goals on March 23, 1994.

The record-breaker came in the second period. The Los Angeles Kings were on the attack against the Vancouver Canucks. Kings defenseman Marty McSorley had the puck on the left side. He spotted Gretzky streaking down the ice on the right. McSorley slid a pass across the ice, right to the stick of Gretzky. Gretzky held it for a second, then slapped it into the goal. Number 802! The crowd went wild, knowing they had just **witnessed** NHL history.

All-Time Goal-Scorers

Wayne Gretzky is the NHL's all-time goal-scorer. Check out this list of the top 10 goal-scorers in NHL history, through 2020.

894	Wayne Gretzky	717	Phil Esposito
801	Gordie Howe	708	Mike Gartner
766	Jaromír Jágr	706	Alex Ovechkin
741	Brett Hull	694	Mark Messier
731	Marcel Dionne	692	Steve Yzerman

Wayne Gretzky (99) scores his 802nd goal (top) and then lifts his hands in the air to soak in his record-breaking moment in front of a roaring crowd (left).

Kane's Hidden Goal

Almost no one even saw one of the biggest goals in NHL history. It came in Game 6 of the 2010 Stanley Cup Finals. The Chicago Blackhawks and the Philadelphia Flyers were locked in a 3–3 overtime tie. Chicago needed a goal to win their first Stanley Cup in almost 50 years.

In overtime, Patrick Kane controlled the puck along the left side. He skated wide, almost **parallel** to the goal. It was a nearly impossible shooting angle. But Kane took a shot anyway.

The shot really didn't look like much. The puck came loose in front of the goal, and Philly started skating the other way. Then, suddenly, the officials blew the whistle. The horn sounded. It was a goal! The puck had barely crossed over the goal line for a fraction of a second. The goal clinched the Stanley Cup for Chicago, and almost nobody had even seen it go in!

Almost no one on the ice or in the stands spotted Patrick Kane's (88) game-winning goal to clinch the 2010 Stanley Cup.

Ovechkin Scores from His Back

Alex Ovechkin of the Washington Capitals may be the greatest goal-scorer of his era. One of his most amazing goals came on January 16, 2006.

Ovechkin carried the puck into the Phoenix Coyotes zone and skated toward the goal. But the defense was all over him. A heavy check knocked Ovechkin to his back. He was sliding on his back, with one hand on his stick. Yet, somehow, he brought the stick around and flipped the puck into the goal.

FACT

Joe Malone is the only NHL player to score seven goals in a single game. Playing for the Quebec Bulldogs, he did it on January 31, 1920.

The shot was one part luck and one part skill. And even today, Ovechkin calls it the greatest goal he ever scored.

Alex Ovechkin shoots the puck (just out of frame) while sliding on his back to make an unbelievable goal.

GLOSSARY

acrobatic (AK-ruh-bat-ik)—having to do with movements borrowed from gymnastics, like handstands, flips, and forward rolls

blue line (BLOO LINE)—one of two lines that mark the start of each offensive zone on a hockey rink

breakaway (BRAKE-uh-way)—a situation in which no defenders stand between an offensive player with the puck and the goal

check (CHEK)—a hard body hit on another player designed to knock the puck free

defenseman (dih-FENS-muhn)—a player who lines up in a defensive zone to prevent opponents from getting open shots on goal

hat trick (HAT TRIK)—three goals by one player in a single game

milestone (MILE-stone)—an important event or development

one-timer (won-TIME-ur)—a hard shot made on a moving puck

overtime (OH-vur-time)—an extra period played if the score is tied at the end of a game

parallel (PA-ruh-lel)—in a straight line

sudden death (SUHD-uhn DETH)—an overtime period that ends as soon as either team scores

witness (WIT-niss)—to see or hear something

READ MORE

Fishman, Jon M. *Hockey's G.O.A.T.: Wayne Gretzky, Sidney Crosby, and More.* Minneapolis: Lerner Publications, 2020.

Hewson, Anthony K. *Hockey Records.* Lake Elmo, MN: Focus Readers, 2020.

Williams, Heather. *Hockey: A Guide for Players and Fans.* North Mankato, MN: Capstone Press, 2020.

INTERNET SITES

Hockey Reference
www.hockey-reference.com

National Hockey League
www.nhl.com

Sports Illustrated Kids: Hockey
www.sikids.com/hockey

INDEX

All-Star Game, 22
all-time goal-scorers, 18, 24
Arnott, Jason, 10–11

baseball-style goals, 19
between-the-legs goals, 14

called-shot goals, 22
Canada, 12
Crosby, Sidney, 12, 18–19

Eruzione, Mike, 8, 9

goalie goals, 20
goalies, 4, 20
Gretzky, Wayne, 24

hat tricks, 22
Hextall, Ron, 20

Kane, Patrick, 27

lacrosse-style goals, 16

Malone, Joe, 28
Milano, Sonny, 14

Miracle on Ice, 9

National Women's Hockey
   League, 18
Nolan, Owen, 22

Orr, Bobby, 6–7
Ovechkin, Alex, 28–29
overtime, 5, 6, 10, 12, 26, 27

playoffs, 5, 18–19, 20

record-breaking goals, 24

Soviet Union, 8
Stanley Cup, 6–7, 10–11, 21,
   26, 27
Svechnikov, Andrei, 16

Team USA, 8–9, 12

Winter Olympics, 8–9, 12